All About Schools

by Jesse McDermott

Editorial Offices: Glenview, Illinois • Parsippany, New Jersey • New York, New York
Sales Offices: Needham, Massachusetts • Duluth, Georgia • Glenview, Illinois
Coppell, Texas • Ontario, California • Mesa, Arizona

Every effort has been made to secure permission and provide appropriate credit for photographic material. The publisher deeply regrets any omission and pledges to correct errors called to its attention in subsequent editions.

Unless otherwise acknowledged, all photographs are the property of Scott Foresman, a division of Pearson Education.

Photo locators denoted as follows: Top (T), Center (C), Bottom (B), Left (L), Right (R), Background (Bkgd)

Opener ©Bettmann/Corbis; 1 ©Bettmann/Corbis; 5 Getty Images; 6 ©Bettmann/Corbis; 8 ©Paul Almasy/Corbis; 9 ©Nano Calvo - V&W/The Image Works, Inc.; 10 North Wind Picture Archives; 11 The Granger Collection, NY; 13 North Wind Picture Archives; 15 ©Hulton Archive/Getty Images; 19 ©Bettmann/Corbis; 20 ©Bettmann/Corbis; 22 ©Jim Cummins/Corbis

ISBN: 0-328-13666-2

Copyright © Pearson Education, Inc.

All Rights Reserved. Printed in the United States of America. This publication is protected by Copyright, and permission should be obtained from the publisher prior to any prohibited reproduction, storage in a retrieval system, or transmission in any form by any means, electronic, mechanical, photocopying, recording, or likewise. For information regarding permission(s), write to: Permissions Department, Scott Foresman, 1900 East Lake Avenue, Glenview, Illinois 60025.

6 7 8 9 10 V0G1 14 13 12 11 10 09 08

CONTENTS

INTRODUCTION 4

CHAPTER 1
The Earliest Schools 4

CHAPTER 2
Greek and Roman Schools 6

CHAPTER 3
Schools in Colonial America 9

CHAPTER 4
The Roots of Common Schools 12

CHAPTER 5
The Birth of Common Schools 14

CHAPTER 6
School Reform in the Twentieth Century 18

SUMMARY 21

NOW TRY THIS 22

GLOSSARY 24

Introduction

When you think about school, perhaps you picture the way your school building looks from the outside or the way your classrooms look from the inside. If you've been to more than one school, you've probably noticed that they are very similar in many ways or that they use the same kinds of tools.

You might think that schools have always been this way. But schools can look very different in other countries. Even in the United States, schools did not always appear or function as they do today. The story of our modern public school system dates back to the ancient Greeks, who lived thousands of years ago. Schools have gone through a lot of changes since then.

If you could go back to ancient Greece, you would not find anything like the school you attend now. This book will tell you what schools were like in those early days, as well as how the modern American school system developed from those roots.

Chapter 1
The Earliest Schools

Throughout history, people have found ways to pass on information to the next generation. In early times, children would learn hunting and fishing techniques and survival skills by watching adults and copying them. Through trial-and-error, the young men and women learned the skills they would need to survive. In addition, children were taught about cultural and religious traditions.

As civilizations progressed in the ancient world, so did the ways in which people were taught. In early India, young children were taught by their families about the laws, traditions, and customs of their country. Then they attended village schools, where they memorized and copied religious books and learned to write on strips of palm leaves.

The first schools were usually located at religious centers, and learning in those days was almost always religious. Children were taught how to read so that they could read the sacred books.

In ancient Jewish tradition, schools were located in or near a synagogue—an institution of prayer. At the age of six, children began attending elementary school at the local synagogue.

At early synagogue schools, children not only learned to read and write, they learned their traditions. This boy is learning to blow the shofar, a trumpetlike horn made from a ram's horn and used to call people together.

Chapter 2
Greek and Roman Schools

Ancient Greek civilization has had a significant influence on many subsequent societies, especially in the area of education. At the height of their civilization, Greek schools were designed to prepare young men for their lives as Greek citizens.

In the city-state of Athens, children began to go to school at age seven. They attended two schools—one for physical exercise and another for music, reading, writing, and other subjects. Children learned how to read and write at first by tracing the alphabet with a stick in the sand. When they had mastered this skill, children were instructed to copy the manuscripts of famous authors. Eventually, they would progress to tracing the words on wax tablets and, finally, to writing in ink on **parchment**.

At the age of fifteen, young men went to a gymnasium, where they had advanced physical training and studied public speaking, debate, and politics to prepare for their adulthood as citizens.

After Greece became part of the Roman Empire in 146 B.C., Roman schools began to develop. Before this time, education in Rome had been conducted mostly in the home, where children learned to read and write or prepare for a trade. But after Greek culture was **absorbed** into Roman culture, a three-tiered school system was established.

The ancient Greeks were among the first people to think that education includes more than just learning history and traditions.

The young Roman's education began at the elementary school, where he studied reading, writing, and basic mathematics. At first, children learned to read from Roman history, poetry, and religious songs, but as the influence of the Greek culture spread, Roman children began reading the classic Greek stories too. The young Roman continued with advanced work at the grammar school. Finally, as in Greece, the last school prepared him to speak in public and instructed him in political and legal matters.

The Roman school system was important in another way: it was among the first school systems to be subsidized, or paid for, by the government. The Roman emperors also helped the school system by paying teachers or excusing them from paying taxes, or by giving scholarships to students. By the end of the Roman Empire, the schools were controlled completely by the government. This was the first "public" school system.

Public institutions of the 19th and 20th centuries—such as this Hellenic Academy in Athens, Greece—were often constructed according to Greek architectural ideals.

Chapter 3
Schools in Colonial America

The world of ancient education had an influence on the growth of the Colonial American school system. Of course, methods of education went through many changes during the centuries in between.

Many of the first colonists of the New World were English and had been brought up in England's schools. It is not surprising that when the English established colonies in America, they created schools like the ones they had themselves attended as children. There were three different kinds of school systems in the colonies, which actually **originated** during medieval times.

Oldest wood schoolhouse in the United States
St. Augustine, Florida

In the Southern Colonies, such as Georgia and South Carolina, people lived far apart because so much of the land was farmland. This made it difficult to create schools that could serve a large number of children, and, as a result, there were very few elementary schools. Children were taught by their parents, if at all. Advanced schools existed for those who could afford them, but elementary schools were only established when a wealthy patron provided money to build one.

In the Middle Colonies, such as Pennsylvania and New York, there were elementary schools that were basically church schools. These schools mostly taught religion, but in the process the students also learned the traditional subjects.

One-room school in Pennsylvania in the 1700s

The Northern Colonies, such as Massachusetts and New Hampshire, took the first steps toward a public school system that was encouraged and partly paid for by the government. In Massachusetts, some towns had schools that were paid for by the residents and could be attended by anyone. These schools were created when a group of families got together and hired a teacher for their children. The families might build a one-room schoolhouse; then the children learned from whatever books their parents could provide.

There were also advanced schools called grammar schools. These were based on the English schools that many of the colonists had attended. These schools taught Latin grammar, mathematics, sciences, and modern languages. They were mainly designed to prepare students for college, while the other schools focused on teaching reading, writing, and basic mathematics.

American colonial hornbook, 18th century

Chapter 4
The Roots of Common Schools

Despite Massachusetts's support for community-based schools, free schools were not available to everyone for much of America's history. Instead, there were private schools for those who could afford them, including the religious schools. But if parents could not afford those, there were charity schools where children were taught and provided with books for free. The schools were paid for by wealthy patrons who wished to leave a **legacy** after their death.

The quality of education that charity and private schools offered differed greatly. While the private schools offered some variety in their classes, the charity and neighborhood schools taught only basic reading, writing, and math. Conditions in the charity schools were more difficult too. There were very few materials to use. Paper was expensive, and blackboards, pencils, and other educational tools were not available. Instead, students used tree bark or sand to learn writing and math. Even worse, many of the school buildings were in poor shape and had leaky roofs. It was a concern over conditions like these that led to a **movement** for better quality, free schools that would be available to all students.

Pupils reciting poetry in a one-room school

Chapter 5
The Birth of Common Schools

Leading up to the 1840s, the neighborhood-organized schools in Massachusetts grew from a few one-room school houses into a system of district schools. As the state grew, it became difficult to bring the children together in one place, and the small number of teachers meant that schools could not be created in every town.

In response to this problem, a few towns would group together to form a school district. The taxes paid by the residents of the district helped pay for the school. The children from each town in the district attended the district school, which was bigger than the one-room schools, where they were taught the elementary subjects, such as reading, writing, and mathematics, along with some science and history.

The district schools were the seed that the common schools grew from. The government supported the schools by giving money to towns that had organized into districts. This support was a step toward the goal of free education for everyone. In 1837, Massachusetts created a State Board of Education in order to spread information about the new common school system and suggest ways to improve the system.

Horace Mann (1796–1859) became known as the "father of American public school education." His work as secretary of the Board of Education in Massachusetts led to the creation of free schools that were open to the public.

When Horace Mann was a child, his parents could not afford to send him to a private school, so he had attended a district school. His experience led him to feel that education should be free and available to all children.

As secretary of education in Massachusetts, Mann traveled around the state, visiting the many school districts. He found that most schools were one-room houses or log cabins in which poor conditions were common. Heat came from a single fireplace, and there were few windows for fresh air. Blackboards, maps, and globes were scarce.

Mann was appalled at the conditions he saw and made it a **priority** to improve them. Over the years to come, Mann succeeded in moving a number of these schools to a new kind of building. These were much larger, and each had ten or more classrooms, a principal's

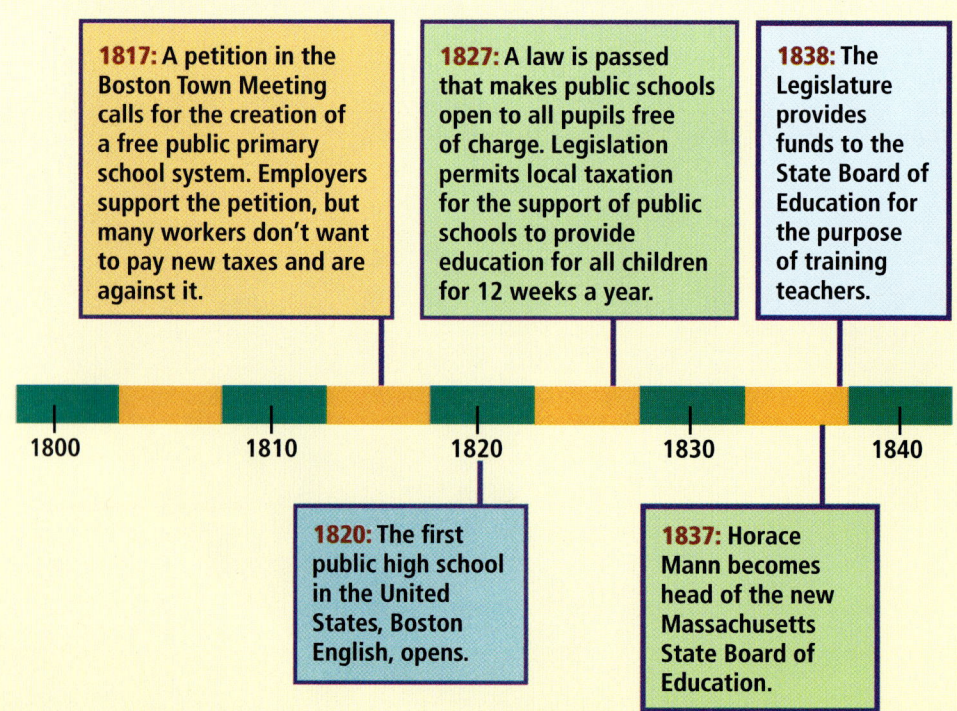

Major Improvements to the Massachusetts School System during the 1800s

1817: A petition in the Boston Town Meeting calls for the creation of a free public primary school system. Employers support the petition, but many workers don't want to pay new taxes and are against it.

1827: A law is passed that makes public schools open to all pupils free of charge. Legislation permits local taxation for the support of public schools to provide education for all children for 12 weeks a year.

1838: The Legislature provides funds to the State Board of Education for the purpose of training teachers.

1820: The first public high school in the United States, Boston English, opens.

1837: Horace Mann becomes head of the new Massachusetts State Board of Education.

office, and even an auditorium. Blackboards, maps, globes, and pens were used regularly, as well.

Mann used his annual reports to argue in support of a common school system. He persuaded wealthy businessmen that it was in their best interest to support the common schools, for their support would benefit themselves as well.

Mann's work led to the establishment of the public school system in Massachusetts. He then traveled around the nation, sharing what he had accomplished in Massachusetts.

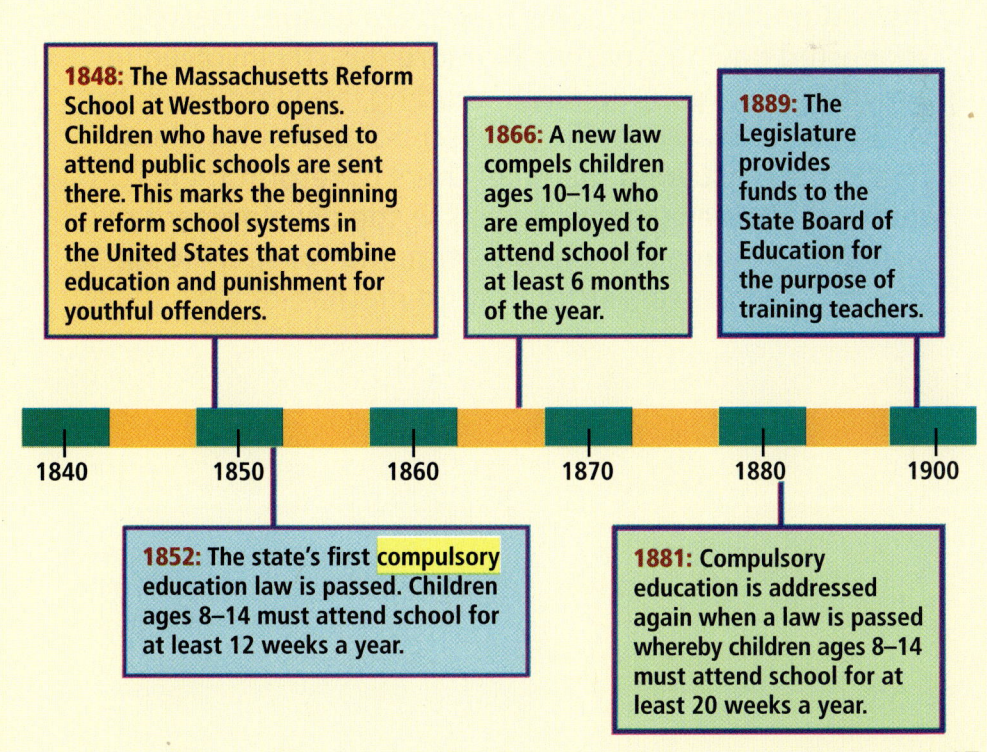

Chapter 6
School Reform in the Twentieth Century

By the last decades of the nineteenth century, the common school system had spread through most of the country. Every state's constitution guaranteed some kind of support for public schools. At the start of the twentieth century, there were about 16 million children in public elementary schools.

Many of these schools looked and functioned much like the English grammar schools that the colonists brought to America. Students sat in rows listening to their teacher recite a lesson, which the students then had to copy and memorize. People began to realize that this method was not necessarily the best way to teach students.

John Dewey was a philosopher and educator who believed that students learn best when they actively experience what they are supposed to learn. For example, instead of making students memorize lessons, Dewey suggested having students be more directly involved in activities that required math, reading, and writing skills.

Dewey ran an experimental school to test his ideas. Its success persuaded many teachers to reform their methods. Dewey's ideas also led to the development of vocational training in schools—training for specific kinds of work, such as carpentry or auto mechanics.

John Dewey (1859–1952) was responsible for many changes in the way students are taught.

Schools experienced other important changes during the twentieth century. Some of the changes had to do with a transition away from a society that had used children as part of the work force. Americans realized that children were not small adults and that they all needed to be educated as well as protected.

Other changes had to do with a growing awareness that the different stages of children's lives are unique. Early elementary schools contained grades one through eight, and students then went directly to high school.

Beginning in the twentieth century, junior high schools were introduced to hold grades seven through nine. This change recognized that the needs of children in the early teenage years are very different from those of either younger children or older teenagers.

There were many other education reforms in the twentieth century. One very significant change had to do with who was allowed in the classroom.

School districts had been allowed to operate separate schools for African American and white children. They were supposed to be "separate but equal" in their educational quality; however, they were not equal. African American schools lacked the funding and resources of white schools. A court case challenged these unfair differences. The U.S. Supreme Court ordered that children of different races should be educated together.

Summary

Today, we can see the growth of centuries of school development. The school you're in right now has built on the successes of other schools that came before it. Schools will continue to change in the future.

The 1954 historic Supreme Court decision in the case of *Brown v. Board of Education* ordered the integration of American schools.

Now Try This

Using what you have learned, try to come up with a plan for creating your own school. Start by answering the questions that follow and then add any other ideas of your own.

Here's How To Do It!

1. Decide what subjects your school will teach. Will it stick to the same subjects that have been taught in elementary school since the time of the Greeks, or do you want to add some more modern ones? What does the next generation of students need to learn?

2. Draw up a plan for what the inside of your school building will look like. How many rooms will there be? What kinds of tools will your students use?

3. Describe the way teachers in your school will teach Think about how they taught throughout this book, and think about what your teachers have done. Which way of teaching will work best for your students?

Glossary

absorbed *v.* taken into.

compulsory *adj.* required.

movement *n.* the efforts and results of a group of people who share a common interest.

originated *v.* began; started.

parchment *n.* paperlike material made from animal skin.

patron *n.* person who gives approval and support to some person, art, cause, or undertaking.

priority *n.* something that is especially important.

Women on the way Up

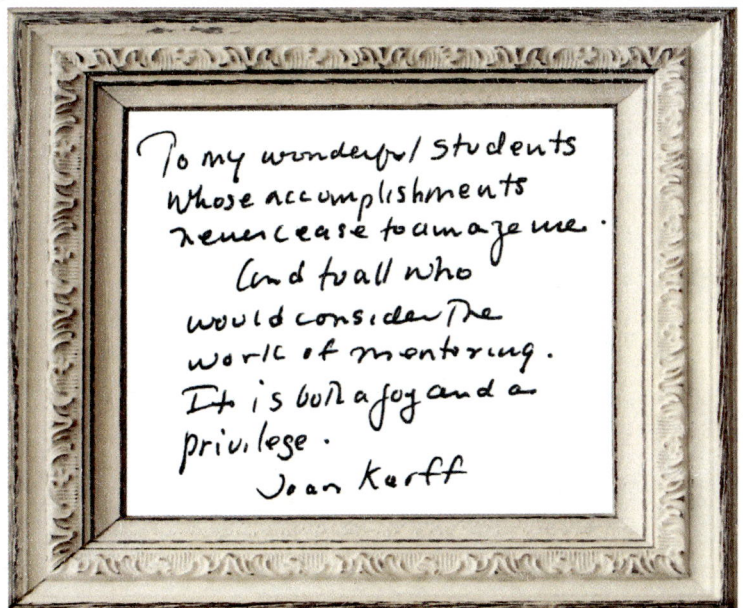

To my wonderful students whose accomplishments never cease to amaze me. And to all who would consider the world of mentoring. It is both a joy and a privilege.

Joan Korff